An audio recording of this book is available at:

ISLAMIC AUDIOBOOKS FORUM

www.islamicaudiobooks.webs.com

Other published and upcoming titles:

The Search for Inner Peace

Did God Become Man?

The True Message of Jesus Christ

Muhammad's Prophethood: An Analytical View

The Best Way to Live and Die

Contents

In the Name of Allaah, the Entirely Merciful, the Especially Merciful

I ask Allaah, the Bountiful Lord of the great Throne to take care of you and protect you in this world and the next, to make you blessed wherever you are and to make you among those who are grateful when provided, patient when tested and who repent when they fall into sin – for indeed, these three are the keys to happiness.

Know, may Allaah guide you to His obedience, that *al-Haneefeeyah* – the religion of Ibraaheem (peace be upon him) is that you worship Allaah alone, sincerely, making your religion pure for Him. Allaah, the Most High, says,

$$\text{﴿ وَمَا خَلَقْتُ ٱلْجِنَّ وَٱلْإِنسَ إِلَّا لِيَعْبُدُونِ ﴾}$$

"I did not create jinn and mankind except to worship Me."

[Soorah adh-Dhaariyaat (51): 56]

Once you know that Allah has created you for His worship, then you should also know that the worship is not acceptable except with *tawheed*, just as salaah is not acceptable without purity.

And once you know that when *shirk* enters worship, the worship becomes unacceptable, the deed is rendered fruitless and the doer is doomed to eternal hellfire, then you will realize that your highest concern should be to study this most important topic, that Allah may save you from this evil trap of *shirk*. Allaah, the Most High, has said:

﴿ إِنَّ ٱللَّهَ لَا يَغْفِرُ أَن يُشْرَكَ بِهِۦ وَيَغْفِرُ مَا دُونَ ذَٰلِكَ لِمَن يَشَآءُ ﴾

"Certainly, Allaah does not forgive the sin of associating others with Him, but He forgives what is less than that for whoever He wills."

[Soorah an-Nisaa' (4): 48 & 116]

And this knowledge consists of four principles that Allaah has mentioned in His Book.

THE FIRST PRINCIPLE

The disbelievers whom the Messenger ﷺ (peace and blessings be upon him) had struggled against, acknowledged that Allaah is the Creator, Sustainer and Controller of the universe. However, this belief alone was not enough to make them Muslims! And proof of their admission of this fact is in Allaah's statement,

> ﴿ قُلْ مَن يَرْزُقُكُم مِّنَ ٱلسَّمَآءِ وَٱلْأَرْضِ أَمَّن يَمْلِكُ ٱلسَّمْعَ وَٱلْأَبْصَـٰرَ وَمَن يُخْرِجُ ٱلْحَىَّ مِنَ ٱلْمَيِّتِ وَيُخْرِجُ ٱلْمَيِّتَ مِنَ ٱلْحَىِّ وَمَن يُدَبِّرُ ٱلْأَمْرَ فَسَيَقُولُونَ ٱللَّهُ فَقُلْ أَفَلَا تَتَّقُونَ ﴾

"Say: Who provides for you from the heaven and the earth? Who owns your hearing and sight? Who brings the living out of the dead and the dead out of the living and who directs the

course of this world?' They will say: Allaah! Say:
Will you not then keep your duty to Him?"

[Soorah Yoonus (10): 31]

THE SECOND PRINCIPLE

The Arab pagans claimed that they did not call upon their gods and turn towards them except to gain nearness to Allaah and that their gods may intercede with Allaah on their behalf.

The proof of their seeking nearness to Allaah is Allaah's statement,

﴿ أَلَا لِلَّهِ الدِّينُ الْخَالِصُ وَالَّذِينَ اتَّخَذُوا مِن دُونِهِ أَوْلِيَاءَ مَا نَعْبُدُهُمْ إِلَّا لِيُقَرِّبُونَا إِلَى اللَّهِ زُلْفَى إِنَّ اللَّهَ يَحْكُمُ بَيْنَهُمْ فِي مَا هُمْ فِيهِ يَخْتَلِفُونَ إِنَّ اللَّهَ لَا يَهْدِي مَنْ هُوَ كَاذِبٌ كَفَّارٌ ﴾

"Unquestionably, for Allaah is the pure religion. But those who take protectors besides Him say: We only worship them that they may bring us nearer to Allaah in position! Indeed, Allaah will judge between them concerning that over which they differ. Indeed, Allaah does not guide one who is a liar and unrelenting disbeliever."

[Soorah az-Zumar (39): 3]

And the proof of their seeking intercession is Allaah's statement,

$$\lessgtr \text{وَيَعْبُدُونَ مِن دُونِ ٱللَّهِ مَا لَا يَضُرُّهُمْ وَلَا يَنفَعُهُمْ وَيَقُولُونَ هَٰؤُلَآءِ شُفَعَٰٓؤُنَا عِندَ ٱللَّهِ} \greatless$$

"And they worship other than Allaah; that which neither harms them nor benefits them, and they say: These are our intercessors with Allaah!"

[Soorah Yoonus (10):18]

Intercession is of two types, the negated intercession which is forbidden; and the affirmed intercession which is allowed.

The intercession which is negated involves asking other than Allaah concerning a matter which only Allaah has power over. The proof for this is Allaah's statement,

﴿ يَـٰٓأَيُّهَا ٱلَّذِينَ ءَامَنُوٓاْ أَنفِقُواْ مِمَّا رَزَقۡنَـٰكُم مِّن قَبۡلِ أَن يَأۡتِىَ يَوۡمٌ لَّا بَيۡعٌ فِيهِ وَلَا خُلَّةٌ وَلَا شَفَـٰعَةٌ وَٱلۡكَـٰفِرُونَ هُمُ ٱلظَّـٰلِمُونَ ﴾

"O you who believe, spend from that with which We have provided for you before there comes a Day when there will be no bargaining, no friendship and no intercession. And it is the disbelievers who are the wrongdoers."

[Soorah al-Baqarah (2): 254]

On the other hand, the affirmed intercession is that which is:

❖ asked directly from Allaah;

❖ the intercessor is honoured by being permitted to intercede; and

❖ the one being interceded for is someone whose speech and actions are pleasing to Allaah.

All of these conditions would have to be met before Allaah gives His permission for the intercession, as He states,

$$\left\{ \text{مَن ذَا ٱلَّذِى يَشْفَعُ عِندَهُۥ إِلَّا بِإِذْنِهِۦ} \right\}$$

"Who is there that can intercede with Him,
except by His permission?"

[Soorah al-Baqarah (2): 255]

THE THIRD PRINCIPLE

The Prophet ﷺ appeared among a people who had different objects of worship; some worshipped angels while others worshipped prophets and pious people. Yet others worshipped stones and trees and still others worshipped the sun and the moon. Nevertheless, the Prophet ﷺ fought against them all without making any distinction between them, and the proof is Allaah's statement,

$$﴿ وَقَٰتِلُوهُمْ حَتَّىٰ لَا تَكُونَ فِتْنَةٌ وَيَكُونَ الدِّينُ كُلُّهُ لِلَّهِ ﴾$$

"Fight them until there is no more *fitnah* (i.e., *shirk*) and religion – all of it –becomes for Allaah alone."

[Soorah al-Anfaal (8): 39]

Proof that the sun and the moon were worshipped is Allaah's statement,

﴾ وَمِنْ ءَايَٰتِهِ ٱلَّيْلُ وَٱلنَّهَارُ وَٱلشَّمْسُ وَٱلْقَمَرُ لَا تَسْجُدُواْ لِلشَّمْسِ وَلَا لِلْقَمَرِ وَٱسْجُدُواْ لِلَّهِ ٱلَّذِى خَلَقَهُنَّ ﴿

"And among His signs are the night and the day, and the sun and the moon. Do not prostrate to the sun or the moon but prostrate to Allaah who created them."

[Soorah Fussilat (41): 37]

Proof that the angels were worshipped is Allaah's statement,

﴾ وَلَا يَأْمُرَكُمْ أَن تَتَّخِذُواْ ٱلْمَلَٰئِكَةَ وَٱلنَّبِيِّۦنَ أَرْبَابًا أَيَأْمُرُكُم بِٱلْكُفْرِ بَعْدَ إِذْ أَنتُم مُّسْلِمُونَ ﴿

"Nor would he order you to take angels and prophets as lords. Would he order you to disbelieve after you have submitted to Allaah?"

[Soorah Aali 'Imraan (3): 80]

Proof that the prophets were worshipped is Allaah's statement,

﴿ وَإِذْ قَالَ اللَّهُ يَـٰعِيسَى ابْنَ مَرْيَمَ ءَأَنتَ قُلْتَ لِلنَّاسِ اتَّخِذُونِي وَأُمِّيَ إِلَـٰهَيْنِ مِن دُونِ اللَّهِ قَالَ سُبْحَـٰنَكَ مَا يَكُونُ لِي أَنْ أَقُولَ مَا لَيْسَ لِي بِحَقٍّ إِن كُنتُ قُلْتُهُ فَقَدْ عَلِمْتَهُ تَعْلَمُ مَا فِي نَفْسِي وَلَا أَعْلَمُ مَا فِي نَفْسِكَ إِنَّكَ أَنتَ عَلَّامُ الْغُيُوبِ ﴾

"And (beware the Day) when Allaah will say, O 'Eesaa, Son of Maryam! Did you say to people: Worship me and my mother as gods besides Allaah? He will reply: Exalted are You! It was not for me to say that to which I had no right. Had I said such a thing, You would surely have known it. You know what is in my inner-self while I do not know what is in Yours. Truly, it is only You who is the All-Knower of the unseen."

[Soorah al-Maa'idah (5): 116]

Proof that pious people were worshipped is Allaah's statement,

﴿ أُوْلَٰئِكَ ٱلَّذِينَ يَدْعُونَ يَبْتَغُونَ إِلَىٰ رَبِّهِمُ ٱلْوَسِيلَةَ أَيُّهُمْ أَقْرَبُ وَيَرْجُونَ رَحْمَتَهُۥ وَيَخَافُونَ عَذَابَهُۥٓ ﴾

"Those whom they call upon are themselves seeking an avenue to their Lord, competing in drawing closest to Him, and they hope for His mercy and fear His punishment."

[Soorah al-Israa' (17): 57]

And proof that stones and trees were worshipped is Allaah's statement,

﴿ أَفَرَءَيْتُمُ ٱللَّٰتَ وَٱلْعُزَّىٰ ۝ وَمَنَوٰةَ ٱلثَّالِثَةَ ٱلْأُخْرَىٰٓ ﴾

"Have you considered al-Laat and al-'Uzzaa? And the third one, Manaat?"

[Soorah an-Najm (53): 19-20]

Another proof is the hadeeth of Aboo Waaqid al-Laythee (may Allaah be pleased with him) who narrated,

"We departed with the Prophet ﷺ to Hunain shortly after we had given up disbelief. The polytheists had a tree called Dhaat Anwaat̲, around which they would stand in devotion and hung their weapons upon. When we passed by a tree of the same kind, we said, "O Messenger of Allaah, appoint a tree for us just like they have one." He ﷺ exclaimed,

"Exalted is Allaah! What you have said is like what the Children of Israa'eel said to Moosaa,

$$\text{﴿ٱجۡعَل لَّنَآ إِلَـٰهًا كَمَا لَهُمۡ ءَالِهَةٌ قَالَ إِنَّكُمۡ قَوۡمٌ تَجۡهَلُونَ ﴾}$$

"Make for us a god as they have gods! Moosaa replied: Indeed, You are people who are being ignorant!

[Soorah al-A'raaf (7): 138]

By Him in whose hand is my soul, you will surely follow the ways of those who were before you."[1]

---

[1] Reported by at-Tirmidhee (2180) and graded authentic by

Ibn-ul-Qayyim (*Iqhaathat-ul-Lahfaan*, 2/1054), al-Albaanee (*Hidaayat-ur-Ruwaah*, 5330) and others.

THE FOURTH PRINCIPLE

The *shirk* being committed by those of our time is worse than that which was committed in the pre-Islamic Days of Ignorance. This is because the earlier ones used to commit *shirk* during times of ease but in times of difficulty, they would become sincere in worship. Proof for this is Allaah's statement,

فَإِذَا رَكِبُواْ فِي ٱلْفُلْكِ دَعَوُاْ ٱللَّهَ مُخْلِصِينَ لَهُ ٱلدِّينَ فَلَمَّا نَجَّـٰهُمْ إِلَى ٱلْبَرِّ إِذَا هُمْ يُشْرِكُونَ

"When they embark on a ship they invoke Allaah alone making their faith pure for Him, but when He brings them safely to land, behold, they give a share of their worship to others!"

[Soorah al-'Ankaboot (29): 65]

In contrast, those who associate others with Allaah in the present day are constant in their *shirk*, regardless of ease or hardship!

So based upon this, the case of the polytheists of the Prophet's time against whom he ﷺ struggled appears less severe compared to those of our time, one of the reasons being that the earlier ones used to be sincere in worship – at least – during hardship while the later ones are calling upon their saints all the time, both in prosperity and adversity.

And Allaah knows best.

May Allaah send peace and blessings on Prophet Muhammad, his family and his companions.

<u>About the Author</u>

Imaam Muhammad ibn 'Abd-il-Wahhaab ibn Sulaymaan at-Tameemee was born in 1115 AH (1703 CE) in 'Uyaynah, Arabia [now in Saudi Arabia].

Having completed his formal education in the sacred city of Madinah, in Arabia, under renowned scholar al-'Allaamah Muhammad Hayaat as-Sindee and others, Ibn 'Abd-il-Wahhaab lived abroad for many years. He taught for four years in Basra, Iraq, and in 1736 CE, in Iran, he began to teach against what orthodox scholars of Islam considered to be the extreme ideas of various exponents of Sufi doctrines.

On returning to his native city, he wrote the *Kitaab-ut-Tawheed alladhee huwa Haqqullaahi 'alal-'Abeed* ("Tawheed: The Right of Allaah upon His Slaves"), which is his most famous work.

Ibn 'Abd-il-Wahhaab's teachings have been characterized as puritanical and traditional, representing the earliest era of Islam. He made a clear stand against all innovation in religion (*bid'ah*) because the authentic hadeeths declare it reprehensible without exception. He insisted, like so many others before him, that the original grandeur of Islam could only be regained if the Muslims would return to the creed and methodology enunciated by Prophet Muhammad ﷺ and his companions. He preached against taking intermediaries in worshipping Allaah and condemned any such practice as *shirk* (polytheism) since Allaah is to be invoked directly without any prophet, saint, angel or idol in-between.

Among his well known works are:

- *Thalaathat-ul-Usool* ("Three Fundamental Principles")
- *Kashf-ush-Shubuhaat* ("Clarification of Misunderstandings")

- *Arba' Qawaa'id Tadoorul-Ahkaam 'alaihaa* ("Four Principles which are the Bedrock of Islamic Laws")

He died in 1206 AH (1792 CE), Ad-Dir'īyah.[2]

---

[2] For more details, refer to:

- *Biography and Mission of Muhammad Ibn Abdul Wahhab*, by Jalal Abualrub;
- *The Life, Teachings and Influence of Muhammad Ibn Abdul Wahhaab*, by Jamaal Zarabozo.

Muslims). It is written by Muslim scholars and authors who follow the general methodology of *Ahl-us-Sunnah wal-Jamaa`ah* - the mainstream Muslims.

3. What are some benefits of audiobooks?

They are relatively cheaper and faster to acquire than printed books. They take no physical space, so there is less clutter. No worries about whether to keep, sell off, recycle or give-away. Also, this makes them easier to transport or distribute. It cost the founder of this project thousands of dollars for shipping home just one third of the books in his library after he graduated!

Listening to audiobooks is comfortable and it is a good break for the eyes. You can listen while standing, walking or lying down!

In addition, they support multi-tasking - meaning that you can listen to them while exercising, cleaning around the house, travelling or performing various other activities which you would not be able to do while reading. Of course you can also read when you are travelling (as long as you are not the driver), except that some people (like the present writer) cannot read in a moving car because it makes them dizzy.

Audiobooks also benefit the blind and those with weak or impaired vision. Moreover, foreign and hard-to-pronounce words or names are read correctly for you.

Finally, many (if not most) people today will not (or cannot) just take out time to read! However, audiobooks make their task easier, because instead of sitting with their food in front of the TV everyday, they can just play an audiobook instead!